Divine Rhyme

Divine Rhyme

Edited by
Michael Lester

Live Write Publish Repeat

Contents

Contents

Contents

Contents

"Having" or "Being"

No need to have a Jag – Type E

And have a villa by the sea,

And have clothes with "designer label"

And ave a coat with mink or sable,

And yet, you feel there's something missing!

But wait! Take heart! Here comes a blessing,

To be Free – Just "Be".

- Greta M. Sears -

(My Gran)

You Do Have a Choice

Be happy my friend
For you do have a choice,
You can sit and complain
Or stand and rejoice.
You can waste your life
With judgement and blame,
Or learn to forgive
And understand we're the same.

For all of us feel fear
And everyone knows pain,
Products of experience,
No one's to blame.
So let go of your past,
Your hurts and your fears,
Cherish each moment
And love life while you're still here.

- Author Unknown

Old Wineskins

How hard is it for narrow-visioned man
To break away from long-held, fond ideas,
To overthrow the teachings of his youth,
To burst asunder Personality
And launch himself upon the Sea of Truth,
And walk upon the waters, free of fears,
Aware this is the only way he can
Make any progress in the realm of Thought,
Or open up the channels of the mind,
At present blocked by so much worldly lore,
By prejudice, convention, and the rest
That education and example store
In him with precepts, all which make him blind
And hide from him the fact of knowing naught.

- Michael Dillon

Leisure

What is this life if, full of care,
We have no time to stand and stare?-

No time to stand beneath the boughs
And stare as long as sheep or cows.

No time to see, when woods we pass,
Where squirrels hide their nuts in grass:

No time to see, in broad daylight,
Streams full of stars, like skies at night:

No time to turn at Beauty's glance,
And watch her feet, how they can dance.

No time to wait till her mouth can
Enrich that smile her eyes began?

A poor life this if, full of care,
We have no time to stand and stare.

- William Henry Davies

Much Madness is divinest Sense

Much Madness is divinest Sense —
To a discerning Eye —
Much Sense — the starkest Madness —
'Tis the Majority
In this, as All, prevail —
Assent — and you are sane —
Demur — you're straightway dangerous —
And handled with a Chain —

- Emily Dickinson

Rapture Divine

When the mind's very being is gone.
Sunk in a conscious sleep,
In a rapture divine and deep,
Itself in the Godhead lost:
It is conquered, ravished, and won!
Set in Eternity's sweep,
Gazing back on the steep,
Knowing not how it was crossed –
To a new world now it is tossed,
Drawn from its former state,
To another, measureless, great,
Where love is drowned in the Sea.

- Jacopone da Todi

My Heart Soars

The beauty of the trees,
The softness of the air,
The fragrance of the grass,
Speaks to me.

The summit of the mountain,
The thunder of the sky,
The rhythm of the sea,
Speaks to me.

The faintness of the stars,
The freshness of the morning,
The dew drop on the flower,
Speaks to me.

The strength of fire,
The taste of salmon,
The trail of the sun,
and the life that never goes away,
They speak to me.

And my heart soars.   - Chief Dan George -

He Who Knows Love

He who knows Love—becomes Love, and his eyes
Behold Love in the heart of everyone,
Even the loveless: as the light of the sun
Is one with all it touches. He is wise
With undivided wisdom, for he lies
In Wisdom's arms. His wanderings are done,
For he has found the Source whence all things run—
The guerdon of the quest, that satisfies.

He who knows Love becomes Love, and he knows
All beings are himself, twin-born of Love.
Melted in Love's own fire, his spirit flows
Into all earthly forms, below, above;
He is the breath and glamour of the rose,
He is the benediction of the dove.

- Elsa Barker

Clouds

I'm laughing at the moon

Just hanging there

Lighting up the sky

Wondering what moves all this

As the clouds pass by

Thinking

bird's-eye

What moves all this

Must move I

Or is it true

That all this

Is I?

- Michael Lester -

Thy Guru's Feet

Thy body may be beautiful
and glow with flawless health,
Thy fame colossal
and thou mayest have won to fabulous wealth,
But if to the Guru's feet
thy heart untethered still remain.
Then all thou hast achieved
on earth is vain, is vain, is vain.
Thou mayest be deep-versed
in all that scripture have to tell
A beacon of light,
a master of prose and verse delectable,
But if to the Guru's feet
thy heart untethered still remain.
Then all thou hast achieved on earth
is vain, is vain, is vain.

- Shankaracharya

Life and Death

Life, death, — death, life; the words have led for ages
Our thought and consciousness and firmly seemed
Two opposites; but now long-hidden pages
Are opened, liberating truths undreamed.
Life only is, or death is life disguised, —
Life a short death until by life we are surprised.

- Sri Aurobindo

Give All to Love

Give all to love;
Obey thy heart;
Friends, kindred, days,
Estate, good-fame,
Plans, credit and the Muse,—
Nothing refuse.

'T is a brave master;
Let it have scope:
Follow it utterly,
Hope beyond hope:
High and more high
It dives into noon,
With wing unspent,
Untold intent:
But it is a god,
Knows its own path
And the outlets of the sky.

Divine Rhyme

It was never for the mean;
It requireth courage stout.
Souls above doubt,
Valor unbending,
It will reward,—
They shall return
More than they were,
And ever ascending.

Leave all for love;
Yet, hear me, yet,
One word more thy heart behoved,
One pulse more of firm endeavor,—
Keep thee to-day,
To-morrow, forever,
Free as an Arab
Of thy beloved...

- Ralph Waldo Emerson

If Only

Don't be an "If Only"
You'll wish your life away!
Being "richer", "wiser", "thinner"
Doesn't always "make your day"!

Don't be an "If Only"
Make the most of what is sent,
So, whatever your situation,
Be Happy! — Be Content!

- Greta M. Sears

Nirvana

All is abolished but the mute Alone.
The mind from thought released, the heart from grief
Grow inexistent now beyond belief;
There is no I, no Nature, known-unknown.
The city, a shadow picture without tone,
Floats, quivers unreal; forms without relief
Flow, a cinema's vacant shapes; like a reef
Foundering in shoreless gulfs the world is done.

Only the illimitable Permanent
Is here. A Peace stupendous, featureless, still,
Replaces all, — what once was I, in It
A silent unnamed emptiness content
Either to fade in the Unknowable
Or thrill with the luminous seas of the Infinite.

- Sri Aurobindo

The Master

He fumbles at your Soul
As Players at the Keys
Before they drop full Music on —
He stuns you by degrees —
Prepares your brittle Nature
For the Ethereal Blow
By fainter Hammers — further heard —
Then nearer — Then so slow
Your Breath has time to straighten —
Your Brain — to bubble Cool —
Deals — One — imperial — Thunderbolt —
That scalps your naked Soul —

When Winds take Forests in the Paws —
The Universe — is still —

- Emily Dickinson

A Song

Lord, when the sense of thy sweet grace
Sends up my soul to seek thy face.
Thy blessed eyes breed such desire,
I dy in love's delicious Fire.
O love, I am thy Sacrifice.
Be still triumphant, blessed eyes.
Still shine on me, fair suns! that I
Still may behold, though still I dy.

Though still I dy, I live again;
Still longing so to be still slain,
So gainfull is such losse of breath.
I dy even in desire of death.
Still live in me this loving strife
Of living Death and dying Life.
For while thou sweetly slayest me
Dead to my selfe, I live in Thee.

- Richard Crashaw

Truth Is One

In long devotion to forms that cheat
Thou hast suffered the days of thy life to fleet:
But outward forms are still passing away,
Changing their fashion from day to day.
Tread not ever on stones that are rough to thy feet;
Nor shift from one branch to another thy seat.
Seek high o'er the sphere of the world thy rest;
In the world of reality make thee a nest.
If Truth be thine object, form-worshippers shun;
For form is manifold, Truth is one.
In number trouble and error lie.
To Unity then for sure refuge fly.
If the might of the foeman oppress thee sore,
Fly to the fortress and fear no more.

- Jami

Invictus

Out of the night that covers me,
　　Black as the pit from pole to pole,
I thank whatever gods may be
　　For my unconquerable soul.

In the fell clutch of circumstance
　　I have not winced nor cried aloud.
Under the bludgeonings of chance
　　My head is bloody, but unbowed.

Beyond this place of wrath and tears
　　Looms but the Horror of the shade,
And yet the menace of the years
　　Finds and shall find me unafraid.

It matters not how strait the gate,
　　How charged with punishments the scroll,
I am the master of my fate,
　　I am the captain of my soul.

- William Ernest Henley

All Things Are Full of God

ALL things are full of God. Thus spoke
  Wise Thales in the days
When subtle Greece to thought awoke
  And soared in lofty ways.
And now what wisdom have we more?
  No sage divining-rod
Hath taught than this a deeper lore,
  ALL THINGS ARE FULL OF GOD.

The Light that gloweth in the sky
  And shimmers in the sea,
That quivers in the painted fly
  And gems the pictured lea,
The million hues of Heaven above
  And Earth below are one,
And every lightful eye doth love
  The primal light, the Sun.

Divine Rhyme

Even so, all vital virtue flows
  From life's first fountain, God;
And he who feels, and he who knows,
  Doth feel and know from God.
As fishes swim in briny sea,
  As fowl do float in air,
From Thy embrace we cannot flee;
  We breathe, and Thou art there.

Go, take thy glass, astronomer,
  And all the girth survey
Of sphere harmonious linked to sphere,
  In endless bright array.
All that far-reaching Science there
  Can measure with her rod,
All powers, all laws, are but the fair
  Embodied thoughts of God.

- John Stuart Blackie

Do Not Stand At My Grave and Weep

Do not stand at my grave and weep;
I am not there. I do not sleep.
I am a thousand winds that blow.
I am the diamond glints on snow.
I am the sunlight on ripened grain.
I am the gentle autumn rain.
When you awaken in the morning's hush
I am the swift uplifting rush
Of quiet birds in circling flight.
I am the soft starlight at night.
Do not stand at my grave and cry,
I am not there; I did not die.

- Mary Elizabeth Frye

Sonnet on a Sleeping World

Awake and yet asleep! The whole world lies
Unconscious of its own unconscious state;
Destructive of itself and blind to fate,
Ignoring all the warnings of the wise.
For here or there a man may waken, rise,
Shake off the shackles ere it be too late,
His mind to master, anger, greed, and hate
Drive out and penetrate the veiled guise
Of man mechanical – his nature true –
Which he perceives, his helplessness he knows;
All others cling to dreams that they can do
Whatever they will – themselves mere puppet shows,
Their strings worked by events, nor do they heed
The call to rouse as slaves from fetters freed.

- Michael Dillon

Last Lines

No coward soul is mine,
No trembler in the world's storm-troubled sphere:
I see Heaven's glories shine,
And faith shines equal, arming me from fear.

O God within my breast,
Almighty, ever-present Deity!
Life—that in me has rest,
As I—undying Life—have power in Thee!

Vain are the thousand creeds
That move men's hearts: unutterably vain;
Worthless as wither'd weeds,
Or idlest froth amid the boundless main,

To waken doubt in one
Holding so fast by Thine Infinity;
So surely anchor'd on
The steadfast rock of immortality.

Divine Rhyme

With wide-embracing love
Thy Spirit animates eternal years,
Pervades and broods above,
Changes, sustains, dissolves, creates, and rears.

Though earth and man were gone,
And suns and universes ceased to be,
And Thou were left alone,
Every existence would exist in Thee.

There is not room for Death,
Nor atom that his might could render void:
Thou—Thou art Being and Breath,
And what Thou art may never be destroyed.

- Emily Brontë

Searching

Searching, Searching, o'er the ages,
Countless, endless, written pages
Words of Wisdom, words of learning,
To a soul forever yearning
For the Truth, The Way, The Life.
Soul in conflict, soul in strife.

....

Give up striving, it's a fact,
Let go! Listen! Let God act!
When the going gets too tough –
"Lo, I am with You" – That is enough.

\- Greta M. Sears

High Flight

Oh, I have slipped the surly bonds of earth
And danced the skies on laughter-silvered wings.
Sunward I've climbed and joined the tumbling mirth
Of sun-split clouds – and done a hundred things
You have not dreamed of; wheeled and soared and swung
High in the sunlit silence. Hovering there
I've chased the shouting wind along, and flung
My eager craft through footless halls of air;
Up, up the long delirious burning blue
I've topped the windswept heights with easy grace,
Where never lark nor even eagle flew;
And while, with silent lifting mind I've trod
The high, untrespassed sanctity of space
Put out my hand and touched the face of God.

- Fl. Officer John Gillespie Magee Jr

The Living God

He who is in you and outside you,
Who works through all hands,
Who walks on all feet,
Whose body are all ye,
Him worship, and break all other idols!

He who is at once the high and low,
The sinner and the saint,
Both God and worm,
Him worship – visible, knowable, real, omnipresent,
Break all other idols!

In whom is neither past life
Nor future birth nor death,
In whom we always have been
And always shall be one,
Him worship. Break all other idols!

Divine Rhyme

Ye fools! who neglect the living God,
And His infinite reflections with which the world is
full.

While ye run after imaginary shadows,
That lead alone to fights and quarrels,
Him worship, the only visible!
Break all other idols!

- Swami Vivekananda

The Order of Pure Intuition

HAIL, sacred Order of eternal Truth!
　That deep within the soul,
In axiomatic majesty sublime,
　One undivided whole,—

Up from the underdepth unsearchable
　Of primal Being springs,
An inner world of thought, co-ordinate
　With that of outward things!

Hail, Intuition pure! whose essences
　The central core supply
Of conscience, language, science, certitude,
　Art, beauty, harmony!

Great God! I thank Thy majesty supreme,
　Whose all-creative grace
Not in the sentient faculties alone
　Has laid my reason's base;

Divine Rhyme

Not in abstractions thin by slow degrees
  From grosser forms refin'd;
Not in tradition, nor the broad consent
  Of conscious humankind;—

But in th' essential Presence of Thyself,
  Within the soul's abyss;
Thyself, alike of her intelligence
  The fount, as of her bliss;

Thyself, by nurture, meditation, grace,
  Reflexively reveal'd;
Yet ever acting on the springs of thought,
  E'en when from thought conceal'd!

- Edward Caswall

A Service of Song

Some keep the Sabbath going to Church —
I keep it, staying at Home —
With a Bobolink for a Chorister —
And an Orchard, for a Dome.

Some keep the Sabbath in Surplice —
I just wear my Wings —
And instead of tolling the Bell, for Church,
Our little Sexton sings.

God preaches, a noted Clergyman —
And the sermon is never long,
So instead of getting to Heaven, at last —
I'm going, all along.

- Emily Dickinson

Eyes Expanded

Eyes expanded,
Mind illuminated.
Is this imagined?
Is this fated?

Is this it,
Is this just a glimpse?
Nothing in the world matters,
But this.

Intuition, that there is no 'I',
Life is looking at itself through its own eyes.

And all is well in this soup of peace,
For all but a moment did the person cease?

- Michael Lester

She Was a Phantom of Delight

She was a phantom of delight
When first she gleam'd upon my sight;
A lovely apparition, sent
To be a moment's ornament;
Her eyes as stars of twilight fair;
Like twilight's, too, her dusky hair;
But all things else about her drawn
From Maytime and the cheerful dawn;
A dancing shape, an image gay,
To haunt, to startle, and waylay.
I saw her upon nearer view,
A Spirit, yet a Woman too!
Her household motions light and free,
And steps of virgin liberty;
A countenance in which did meet
Sweet records, promises as sweet;
A creature not too bright or good
For human nature's daily food;
For transient sorrows, simple wiles,
Praise, blame, love, kisses, tears, and smiles.

Divine Rhyme

And now I see with eye serene
The very pulse of the machine;
A being breathing thoughtful breath,
A traveller between life and death;
The reason firm, the temperate will,
Endurance, foresight, strength, and skill;
A perfect Woman, nobly plann'd,
To warm, to comfort, and command;
And yet a Spirit still, and bright
With something of angelic light.

- William Wordsworth

Lord Thou Hast Shown Me

Lord, Thou hast shown me now,
In Thy fair holiness,
Mine utter nothingness;
Yea, less than nothing I!
And from this gazing springs
An eager humbleness;
Prisoned in wretchedness,
My will but lives to die.
My mind's humility
Is not made vile by ill,
But loving virtue still,
Through vileness, gains Thy height.

I cannot be re-born
Till mine own self be dead;
My life out-poured, out-shed,
Sheer essence to renew:
On glorious Nothingness
He only can be fed,
Whom God Himself hath led;
Here man hath naught to do.

Divine Rhyme

O glorious state and true!
In nothingness to cease,
Desire and mind at peace
In calmness infinite.

Ah! how my earth-bound thoughts
Are hideous and mean,
Beside those heights serene,
Where virtue's treasures be.
That deep whereon I gaze,
I cannot swim therein,
I must be swallowed clean,
Like men who drown at sea.
Shoreless Infinity!
I sink in Thee, the Whole:
Thy fulness storms my soul,
Thou sweetness and Thou Light!

- Jacopone da Todi

Celestial Love

Love's hearts are faithful, but not fond,
Bound for the just, but not beyond;
Not glad, as the low-loving herd,
Of self in others still preferred,
But they have heartily designed
The benefit of broad mankind.
And they serve men austerely,
After their own genius, clearly,
Without a false humility;
For this is love's nobility,
Not to scatter bread and gold,
Goods and raiment bought and sold,
But to hold fast his simple sense,
And speak the speech of innocence,
And with hand, and body, and blood,
To make his bosom-counsel good:
For he that feeds men, serveth few,
He serves all, who dares be true.

- from Ralph Waldo Emerson, Celestial Love

Love's Philosophy

The fountains mingle with the river,
  And the rivers with the ocean;
The winds of heaven mix forever
  With a sweet emotion;
Nothing in the world is single;
  All things by a law divine
In another's being mingle–
  Why not I with thine?

See, the mountains kiss high heaven,
  And the waves clasp one another;
No sister flower could be forgiven
  If it disdained its brother;
And the sunlight clasps the earth,
  And the moonbeams kiss the sea;–
What is all this sweet work worth,
  If thou kiss not me?

- Percy Bysshe Shelley

Ever The Same Again

Ever the same again,
My lost Truth rediscovered.
Ever the same again.

Ever the same again,
My forgotten Self remembered.
Ever the same again.

Ever the same again,
My lost Goal regained.
Ever the same again.

- Sri Chinmoy

Never The Same...

Never the same again,
Lost peace restored.
Never the same again.

Never the same again,
Lost joy regained.
Never the same again.

Never the same again,
Lost power reborn.
Never the same again.

- Sri Chinmoy

Immortality

I feel in all my limbs His boundless Grace;
Within my heart the Truth of life shines white.
The secret heights of God my soul now climbs;
No dole, no sombre pang, no death in my sight.

No mortal days and nights can shake my calm;
A Light above sustains my secret soul.
All doubts with grief are banished from my deeps,
My eyes of light perceive my cherished Goal.

Though in the world, I am above its woe;
I dwell in an ocean of supreme release.
My mind, a core of the One's unmeasured thoughts;
The star vast welkin hugs my Spirit's peace.

My eternal days are found in speeding time;
I play upon His Flute of rhapsody.
Impossible deeds no more impossible seem;
In birth chains now shines Immortality.

- Sri Chinmoy

Heaven or Hell?

And when you take that step beyond,
Beyond the veil, beyond the tears,
What awaits? How can one tell?
The fears or hopes of living years?

The fear of darkness, pain and hell,
The fear of everlasting void;
Or hope that at last to dwell
In regions of perpetual Joy?

But what is Hell and where is Hell
And Heaven – where is that place?
Hell is separation from God
And Heaven – full knowledge of His grace.

- Greta M. Sears

My Religion

You ask me "what is my religion"?
Now what if I say I have None?
You'll be wrongly impressed,
And unduly distressed
So wait - I have only begun.

My creed in the sense that you mean it,
Has no single symbol, or sign.
Big, impressive, or small,
There is good in them all,
So perhaps Your religion is mine.

My doctrine is any that stands for
The honor and virtue of men.
For whatever we preach,
We're all striving to reach
A mutual goal in the end.

Divine Rhyme

My church is the one that is nearest
Wherever I happen to be.
The place where men go
Their devotion to show,
Is good - and sufficient for me.

What matters the Name on the mileposts
That stand by the path you have trod?
If the pathway leads UP
Then at last you shall sup
With the infinite army of God.

- Dale Wimbrow

The Tyger

Tyger! Tyger! burning bright
In the forests of the night,
What immortal hand or eye
Could frame thy fearful symmetry?

In what distant deeps or skies
Burnt the fire of thine eyes?
On what wings dare he aspire?
What the hand, dare seize the fire?

And what shoulder, & what art,
Could twist the sinews of thy heart?
And when thy heart began to beat,
What dread hand? & what dread feet?

What the hammer? what the chain?
In what furnace was thy brain?
What the anvil? what dread grasp
Dare its deadly terrors clasp?

Divine Rhyme

When the stars threw down their spears,
And water'd heaven with their tears,
Did he smile his work to see?
Did he who made the Lamb make thee?

Tyger! Tyger! burning bright
In the forests of the night,
What immortal hand or eye
Dare frame thy fearful symmetry?

- William Blake

A Dream

I thought this heart enkindled lay
   On Cupid's burning shrine:
I thought he stole thy heart away,
   And placed it near to mine.

I saw thy heart begin to melt,
   Like ice before the sun;
Till both a glow congenial felt,
   And mingled into one!

- Thomas Moore

Immortal, Invisible, God Only Wise

Immortal, invisible, God only wise,
in light inaccessible, hid from our eyes,
most blessed, most glorious, the Ancient of Days,
almighty, victorious, thy great name we praise.

Unresting, unhasting, and silent as light,
nor wanting, nor wasting, thou rulest in might,
thy justice like mountains high soaring above
thy clouds, which are fountains of goodness and love.

To all, life thou givest, to both great and small.
In all life thou livest, the true life of all.
We blossom and flourish as leaves on the tree,
and wither and perish, but naught changeth thee.

Great God of all glory, great God of all light,
thine angels adore thee, all veiling their sight.
All praise we would render; O help us to see
'tis only the splendor of light hideth thee.

- Walter C. Smith

So Far, So Near

THOU, so far, we grope to grasp thee—
Thou, so near, we cannot clasp thee—
Thou, so wise, our prayers grow heedless—
Thou, so loving, they are needless!
In each human soul thou shinest,
Human-best is thy divinest.
In each deed of love thou warmest;
Evil into good transformest.
Soul of all, and moving centre
Of each moment's life we enter.

Breath of breathing—light of gladness—
Infinite antidote of sadness;—
All-preserving ether flowing
Through the worlds, yet past our knowing.
Never past our trust and loving,
Nor from thine our life removing.
Still creating, still inspiring,
Never of thy creatures tiring;
Artist of thy solar spaces;
And thy humble human faces;

Divine Rhyme

Mighty glooms and splendours voicing;
In thy plastic work rejoicing;
Through benignant law connecting
Best with best—and all perfecting,
Though all human races claim thee,
Thought and language fail to name thee,
Mortal lips be dumb before thee,
Silence only may adore thee!

- Christopher Pearse Cranch

Who Would True Valour See

Who would true valour see,
let him come hither;
one here will constant be,
come wind, come weather;
there's no discouragement
shall make him once relent
his first avowed intent
to be a pilgrim.

Whoso beset him round
with dismal stories,
do but themselves confound,
his strength the more is.
No lion can him fright:
he'll with a giant fight,
but he will have the right
to be a pilgrim.

Divine Rhyme

Hobgoblin nor foul fiend
can daunt his spirit;
he knows he at the end
shall life inherit.
Then, fancies, fly away;
he'll not fear what men say;
he'll labour night and day
to be a pilgrim.

- John Bunyan

Smiles

Smile a little, smile a little,
    As you go along,
Not alone when life is pleasant,
    But when things go wrong.
Care delights to see you frowning,
    Loves to hear you sigh;
Turn a smiling face upon her,
    Quick the dame will fly.

Smile a little, smile a little,
    All along the road;
Every life must have its burden,
    Every heart its load.
Why sit down in gloom and darkness,
    With your grief to sup?
As you drink Fate's bitter tonic,
    Smile across the cup.

Divine Rhyme

Smile upon the troubled pilgrims
    Whom you pass and meet;
  Frowns are thorns, and smiles are blossoms
    Oft for weary feet.
  Do not make the way seem harder
    By a sullen face,
  Smile a little, smile a little,
    Brighten up the place.

  Smile upon your undone labor;
    Not for one who grieves
O'er his task, waits wealth or glory;
    He who smiles achieves.
Though you meet with loss and sorrow
    In the passing years,
  Smile a little, smile a little,
    Even through your tears.

- Ella Wheeler Wilcox

I Am

I know what the mind never will.
I am alive, yet still.

I am the being of all delight,
I am the source of all in sight.

I am care and judgement free,
I am the one that simply be's.

I am the one who fears not,
I am the one that can never rot.

I am unafraid, true and strong,
I am the one who knows no wrong.

I Am.

- Michael Lester

Each Little Flower That Opens

Each little flow'r that opens,
each little bird that sings,
God made their glowing colors,
God made their tiny wings.

The purple-headed mountain,
the river running by,
the sunset, and the morning
that brightens up the sky;

The cold wind in the winter,
the pleasant summer sun,
the ripe fruits in the garden,
God made them, ev'ry one.

God gave us eyes to see them,
and lips that we might tell
how great is God Almighty,
who has made all things well.

- Cecil Frances Alexander

Amazing Grace

Amazing grace! (how sweet the sound)
That sav'd a wretch like me!
I once was lost, but now am found,
Was blind, but now I see.

'Twas grace that taught my heart to fear,
And grace my fears reliev'd;
How precious did that grace appear,
The hour I first believ'd!

Thro' many dangers, toils and snares,
I have already come;
'Tis grace hath brought me safe thus far,
And grace will lead me home.

The Lord has promis'd good to me,
His word my hope secures;
He will my shield and portion be,
As long as life endures.

Divine Rhyme

Yes, when this flesh and heart shall fail
And mortal life shall cease;
I shall possess, within the veil,
A life of joy and peace.

The earth shall soon dissolve like snow,
The sun forbear to shine;
But God, Who call'd me here below,
Will be for ever mine.

- John Newton

Take My Life and Let It Be

Take my life, and let it be
Consecrated, Lord, to Thee;
Take my moments and my days,
Let them flow in ceaseless praise.
Let them flow in ceaseless praise.

Take my hands, and let them move
At the impulse of Thy love;
Take my feet, and let them be
Swift and beautiful for Thee.
Swift and beautiful for Thee.

Take my voice, and let me sing
Always, only, for my King;
Take my lips, and let them be
Filled with messages from Thee.
Filled with messages from Thee.

Divine Rhyme

Take my silver and my gold:
Not a mite would I withhold;
Take my intellect, and use
Ev'ry pow'r as Thou shalt choose.
Ev'ry pow'r as Thou shalt choose.

Take my will, and make it Thine,
It shall be no longer mine;
Take my heart, it is Thine own,
It shall be Thy royal throne.
It shall be Thy royal throne.

Take my love, my Lord, I pour
At Thy feet its treasure store;
Take myself, and I will be,
Ever, only, all for Thee.
Ever, only, all for Thee.

- Frances R. Havergal

A Suggestion

On reaching Old-age,
You'll find (like me).
That to "live in the moment"
Is the "right place" to be.

Don't look to the future,
It may never arrive,
And looking back – THAT
Brings many a sigh:

So, "Live in the moment",
There's nothing to fear,
Who knows? The "moment"
May last many a year.

- Greta M. Sears

Wild Nights!

Wild Nights - Wild Nights!
Were I with thee,
Wild Nights should be
Our luxury!

Futile - the Winds -
To a Heart in port -
Done with the Compass -
Done with the Chart!

Rowing in Eden -
Ah, the Sea!
Might I but moor - Tonight -
In Thee!

- Emily Dickinson -

The Song Of The River

The snow melts on the mountain
And the water runs down to the spring,
And the spring in a turbulent fountain,
With a song of youth to sing,
Runs down to the riotous river,
And the river flows to the sea,
And the water again
Goes back in rain
To the hills where it used to be.
And I wonder if life's deep mystery
Isn't much like the rain and the snow
Returning through all eternity
To the places it used to know.
For life was born on the lofty heights
And flows in a laughing stream,
To the river below
Whose onward flow
Ends in a peaceful dream.
And so at last,
When our life has passed
And the river has run its course,
It again goes back,

Divine Rhyme

O'er the selfsame track,
To the mountain which was its source.
So why prize life
Or why fear death,
Or dread what is to be?
The river ran
Its allotted span
Till it reached the silent sea.
Then the water harked back
To the mountain-top
To begin its course once more.
So we shall run
The course begun
Till we reach the silent shore.
Then revisit earth
In a pure rebirth
From the heart of the virgin snow.
So don't ask why
We live or die,
Or whither, or when we go,
Or wonder about the mysteries
That only God may know

- William Randolph Hearst

Liberation

I have thrown from me the whirling dance of mind
And stand now in the spirit's silence free;
Timeless and deathless beyond creature-kind,
The centre of my own eternity.

I have escaped and the small self is dead;
I am immortal, alone, ineffable;
I have gone out from the universe I made,
And have grown nameless and immeasurable.

My mind is hushed in a wide and endless light,
My heart a solitude of delight and peace,
My sense unsnared by touch and sound and sight,
My body a point in white infinities.

I am the one Being's sole immobile Bliss:
No one I am, I who am all that is.

- Sri Aurobindo

Enquiry

Is there decision or unfolding?

Is there cause and effect or just flowing?

Is mind interpreting or knowing?

Is mind just another happening - coming and going?

So what's knowing?

And what's doing unfolding?

- Michael Lester -

The Absolute

No mind, no form, I only exist;
  Now ceased all will and thought;
The final end of Nature's dance,
  I am it whom I have sought.

A realm of Bliss bare, ultimate;
  Beyond both knower and known;
A rest immense I enjoy at last;
  I face the One alone.

I have crossed the secret ways of life,
  I have become the Goal.
The Truth immutable is revealed;
  I am the way, the God-Soul.

My spirit aware of all the heights,
  I am mute in the core of the Sun.
I barter nothing with time and deeds;
  My cosmic play is done.

- Sri Chinmoy

Acknowledgements

I would like to give great thanks to the following for granting permission to publish copyrighted material:

Sri Aurobindo Ashram Trust for the poems Liberation, Life and Death, and Nirvana from Collected Poems by Sri Aurobindo.

Sri Chinmoy Centre for The Absolute, Ever The Same Again, Never The Same Again, and Immortality from My Flute by Sri Chinmoy, Agni Press, New York, 1972.

I would also like to give thanks to all the authors of the poems included that are in the Public Domain.

Special thanks to my gran Greta M. Sears - I've never felt like you ever left and now here we are sharing our expressions together in the same book.

To all the readers, much love.

Michael

9 781739 946937